WHY DO WE NEED PLANTS?

Annabel Griffin

Illustrated by Tjarda Borsboom

Picture Credits:
Abbreviations: m-middle, t-top, l-left, r-right, bg-background.

Shutterstock: Bachkova Natalia 18tr; Dennis van de water 20tr; Forestman71 23br;
GUDKOV ANDREY 19tr; Kiran Nagarae 23tr; Knelson20 23mr; Leighton collins 23tl;
Leungchopan 23ml; Pangram 23bl; Skyrpnykov Dmytro 21ml; Tao Jiang 18bl; Visharo
20bl; Yakov Oskanov 19bl.

PUBLIC LIBRARY
MENTOR, OH

HUNGRY TOMATO.

Copyright © 2024 Hungry Tomato Ltd

First published in 2024 by Hungry Tomato Ltd
F15, Old Bakery Studios, Blewetts Wharf, Malpas Road, Truro, Cornwall,
TR1 1QH, UK.

A CIP catalog record for this book is available from the British Library.

ISBN 9781835690079

Printed in China

Discover more at
www.hungrytomato.com

Contents

Words in **BOLD** can be found in the glossary.

What Is a Plant?

Plants are living things that can be found almost everywhere on Earth! There are over 300,000 different types of plants on our planet. How many can you name?

Plants come in all sorts of shapes and sizes, but most of them have the same three parts: stem, roots, and leaves.

Stem

A plant's stem grows above the ground and gives support. It acts as a drinking straw for the plant, carrying water and **nutrients** from the roots to different parts of the plant.

Leaves

Leaves are very important. They help the plant make its own food, to give it energy and help it grow.

Roots

Roots are usually hidden underground. They help to hold the plant in place, like an anchor. They also take up water and nutrients from the soil that the plant needs to grow.

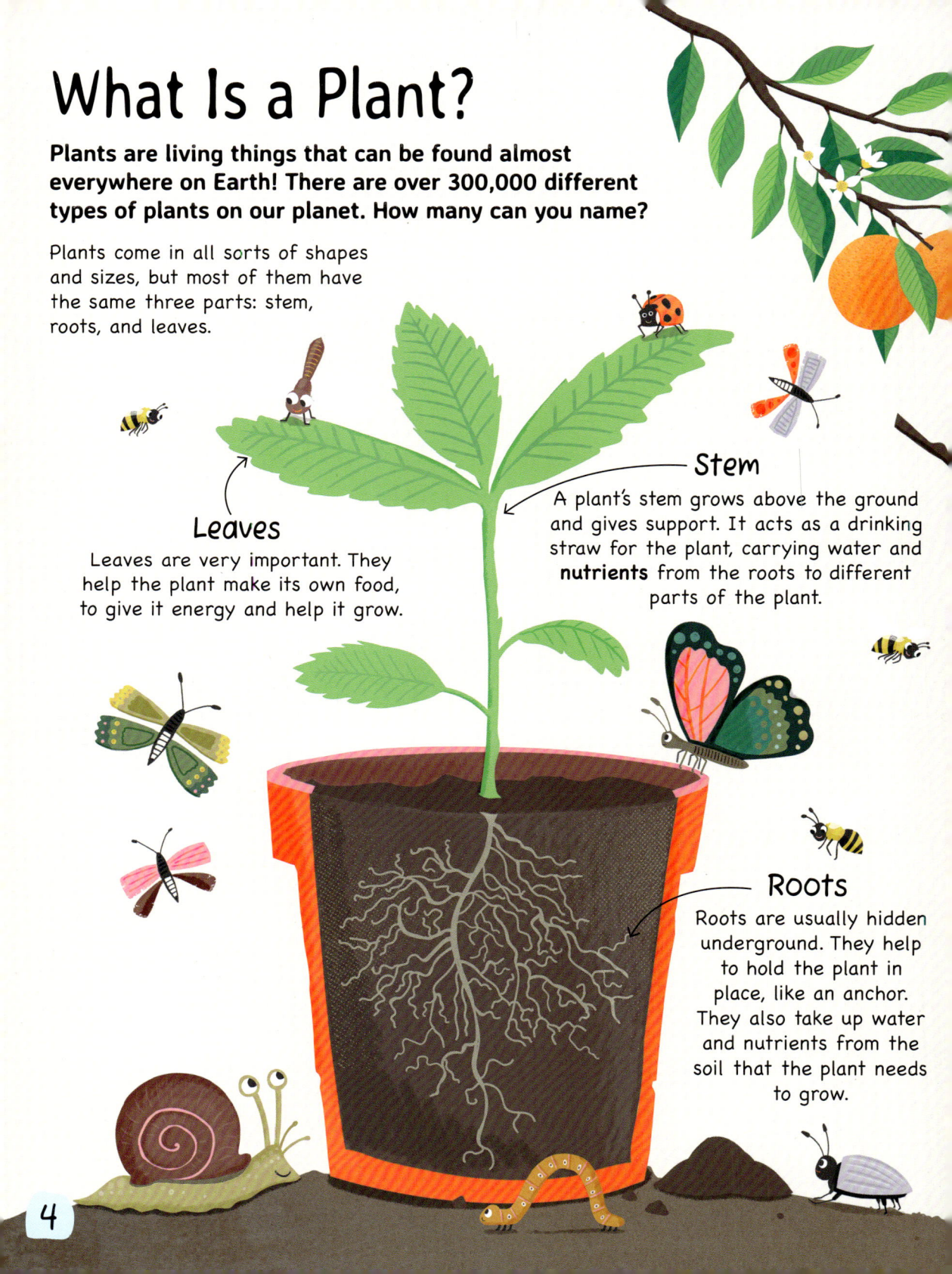

Blossom

Fruit

Berries

Some plants have other features, such as fruit, flowers, thorns, and branches.

Nuts

Flower

Petals

Thorns

Branches

Trunk

Now we know what a plant is, let's find out why they're so important!

Plants at Home

You probably have lots of things made from plants all over your home.

Toiletries

Soap, shampoo, perfume, and make-up often contain parts of plants.

Outside

People with yards often grow plants for decoration, for food, or to help wildlife.

Heating

Wood is sometimes burned for heat.

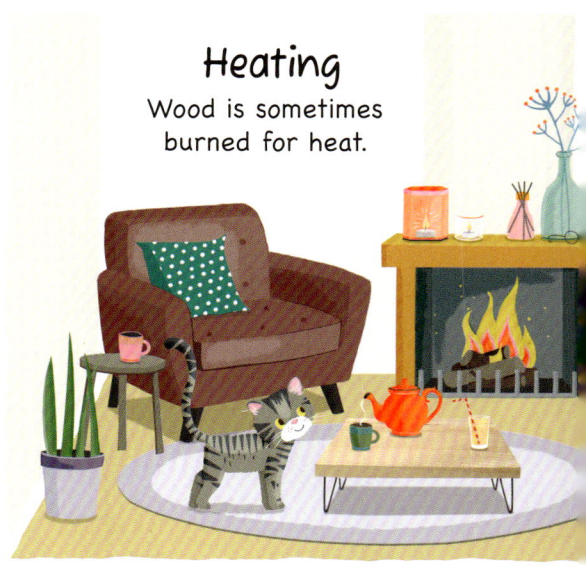

Building
Wood from trees is often used to build parts of houses.

House plants
Having plants inside can make your home look great!

Clothing
Clothing and some fabrics, like cotton, can be made from plants.

Food
Fruits, vegetables, and cereals come from plants.

Books
Paper is made from wood. Without plants, books wouldn't exist!

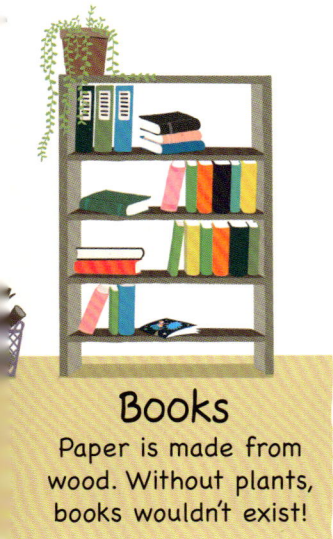

Furniture
Chairs, tables, beds, storage, and other furniture is often made from wood.

7

Useful Plants

Some plants are really handy for turning into useful or beautiful things. Did you know that all of these things are made from plants?

Bamboo

Bamboo is used to make all sorts of things, from houses to toothbrushes. It is fast and easy to grow. Pandas also love it!

Rubber

When a rubber tree's **bark** is cut, it oozes a milky **sap**, called latex. People collect the latex and use it to make rubber. Rubber is used to make all kinds of things, such as balloons.

Perfume

Flowers that smell nice are often used to make perfumes, soaps, and other toiletries.

HAND SOAP

Fabrics

Some plants produce fibers that can be spun into yarn, and used to make fabric.

Linen

Linen is another popular fabric. It's made from flax plants.

Cotton

Cotton plants grow soft, white, fluffy balls of fibers, which can be used to make cotton fabric.

Dyes

Some plants can be used to dye fabrics different colors.

Indigo

The leaves of the indigo plant are used to dye fabrics blue. Denim was traditionally dyed with indigo.

Henna

Leaves from this plant are dried and crushed into a powder to make henna. Henna can be used to dye fabrics, hair, and even skin for special occasions, such as weddings.

9

Good and Bad

People have been using plants to create medicines for centuries. Some plants have the power to both heal and harm, depending on how they are used.

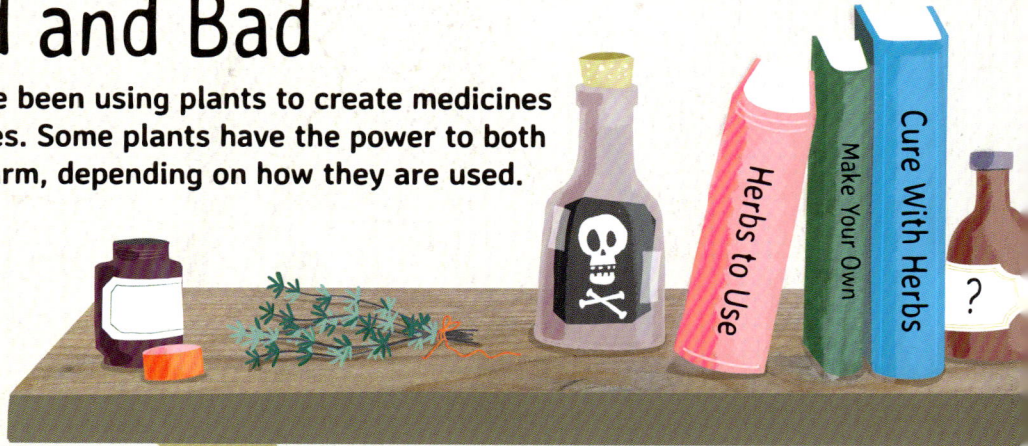

Herbs to Use

Make Your Own

Cure With Herbs

?

Opium poppy

A milky liquid found in these poppies is used to make pain-relief medicine.

Foxgloves

Foxgloves are very poisonous plants, and can make people very sick! However, they also have something in them that can be used as medicine to help treat people with heart failure.

Yew

Yews are **evergreen** trees with red berries. Yew is poisonous, but its bark has been used in medicines to help treat cancer.

Rose periwinkle

This plant grows in Madagascar. It has been used to make medicine to help fight cancer.

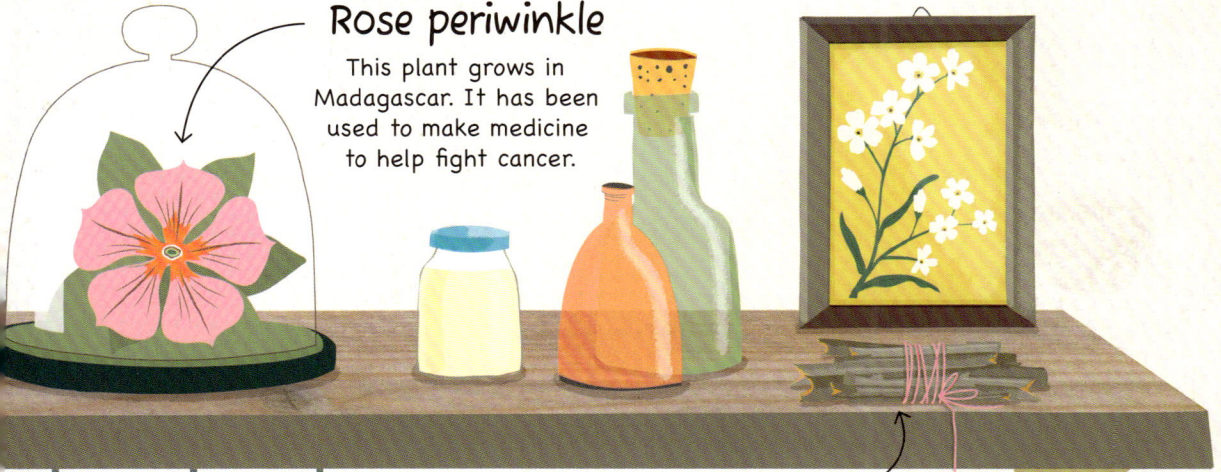

Willow bark

The bark of a willow tree is a natural medicine. It's kind to our bodies and is often used to cure a nasty headache!

Aloe vera

Gel from inside the aloe vera plant can be used to help soothe burns, rashes, and dry skin.

St. John's Wort

St. John's wort has a history of use in herbal medicine dating back to ancient Greece.

11

Feeling Hungry?

Many different plants can be grown for food. Fruits and vegetables are an important part of a healthy diet.

Fruits

Fruits and berries usually grow on trees or bushes. They are often sweet and juicy.

Tomato

That leaf looks tasty!

Leaves

The leaves of some plants, like lettuce, cabbages, and spinach, are great to munch on.

Seeds and pods

Some tasty vegetables, like peas and sweetcorn, are really the seeds of their plant.

Fruit or veg?

Some foods that we call vegetables are actually the fruits of a plant, including pumpkins, cucumbers, and tomatoes.

Roots

Vegetables, such as carrots and beetroot, grow underground. They are the large, tasty roots of the plant.

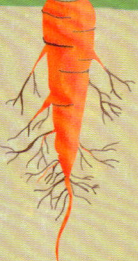

Bulbs

Onions and garlic are actually **bulbs.**

Herbs and Spices

Some plants are used to add extra seasoning or spice. Spices usually come from the seeds, fruit, roots, or bark of a plant, whereas herbs are from the leaves or stems.

Black pepper

Pepper is used to season lots of dishes. Peppercorns are tiny fruit that are usually dried and then crushed or ground into food.

Saffron

Saffron is the most expensive spice in the world. It comes from the flower of the saffron crocus.

Chili pepper

Both the fruit and its seeds can be used to add "heat" and spice to food.

Cinnamon

Cinnamon is a spice that comes from the bark of a cinnamon tree. It is often used in hot drinks and baking.

Ginger

Ginger is a knobbly root that is used in both sweet and savory dishes. It can be used fresh or dried.

14

Chives

Chives are related to onions and garlic. Their leaves have a similar taste, but aren't as strong.

Mint

Lots of things taste like mint. It can also be used as medicine, to settle stomach ache!

Rosemary

Rosemary leaves can be used as a fresh or dried herb.

Rosemary

Chives

PESTO
Alla genovese

Basil

Basil leaves are used in lots of dishes around the world.

Grow Your Own Chive Head

Chives can be used in salads and cooking.

You will need:

- Flowerpot
- Soil/peat-free potting compost
- Chive seeds
- Paints/pens
- Plastic eyes
- Glue
- Scissors

Chive Seeds

1. Decorate your pot using pens or paints, and plastic eyes.

2. Fill your pot with compost and plant your seeds, following the instructions on the seed packet.

3. Put your pot on a tray and place it on a sunny windowsill. Keep it well watered.

4. Once it is over 6 inches (15cm) tall, give your plant a haircut and use the cut chives in your cooking!

15

Planet Savers

Plants play a really important part in keeping our planet healthy.

Clean air

Plants take in **carbon dioxide** from the air and release **oxygen** through their leaves, which humans and other animals need to breathe.

$$CO^2$$

Too much carbon dioxide can lead to **global warming**! Planting more trees and plants will help to stop that happening.

Beautiful world

Plants help to make the world a beautiful place to be! Spending time in nature makes people happy.

Animal habitats

Trees and other plants are perfect **habitats** for animals. They provide food, shelter, and homes.

O^2

Clean water

Plants help to keep water clean by absorbing nutrients that could **pollute** it. Big plants, like trees, help to control the amount of rain that falls, reducing **droughts** and **flooding**.

Healthy soil

Fallen leaves and dead plants add nutrients back into the soil, keeping it healthy so that other plants can grow.

Why Do Animals Need Plants?

Lots of animals rely on plants for their food, homes and shelter. How many can you think of?

Frog homes

Many frogs lay their eggs (called frogspawn) in ponds sheltered by reeds and other plants. This is a safe place for their babies to grow.

High and safe

Birds build their nests in trees to stay safely out of the reach of prowling predators, such as foxes and wolves.

Desert shelters

There's not much shelter in the desert, so Gila woodpeckers and little elf owls make their nests inside cacti.

Clever camouflage

Clever animals, such as chameleons, can change their skin to match their surroundings and stay hidden. They blend in with the leaves they live in.

Plant diets

Lots of animals are **herbivores** which means they only eat plants. Some animals, such as orangutans, mostly eat fruit. Other animals, such as sloths, mostly eat leaves.

Pond protectors

Pond plants provide shelter for fish hiding from predators, such as birds. The plants also filter the water to make it cleaner for the fish to live in.

Grasses and meadows

Many animals, such as lizards and snakes, live among the long grasses of meadows. This is a perfect habitat for them as the grass provides a place to hide from bigger animals.

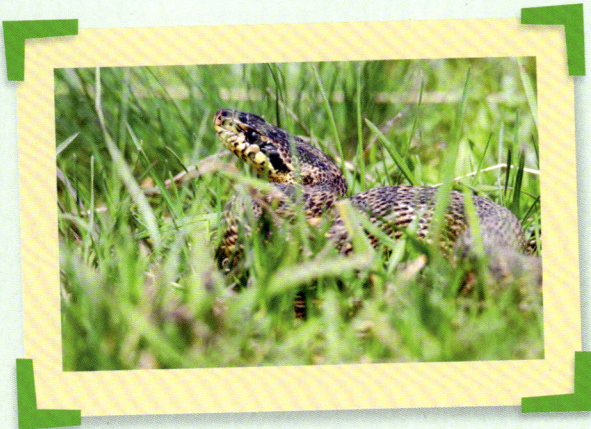

Insect food

Insects, such as bees and butterflies, collect nectar made by flowers. This sugary liquid gives them energy, and is what bees use to make honey. Yum!

Did You Know?

Plants are pretty amazing! Every living creature needs plants to survive; the world wouldn't be the way it is today if we didn't have them. Did you know these amazing facts about plants?

Saffron is the most expensive spice in the world. Sometimes, it can cost more than gold!

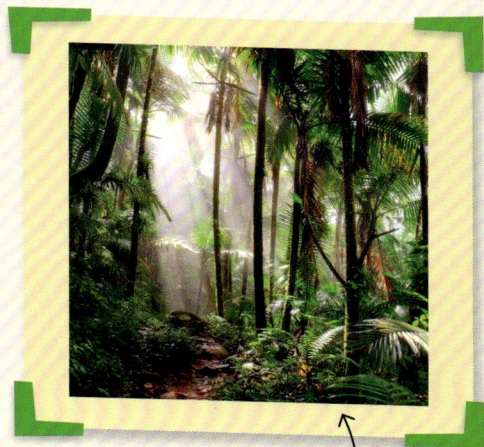

It can take **10** minutes for a falling raindrop to make its way through the rainforest's thick canopy and reach the ground!

70,000 plant species have been used for medicine!

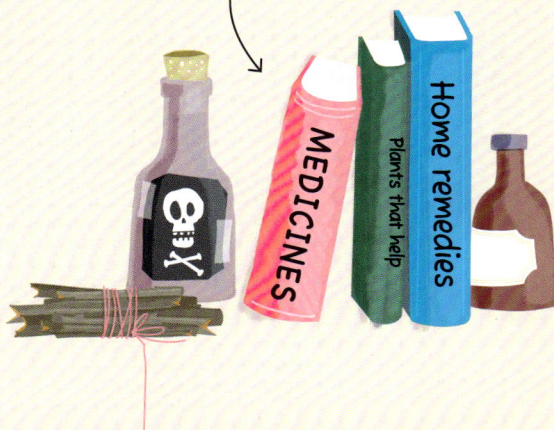

Bluebell plant

The sap from bluebell plants was once used as glue to hold books together.

MEDICINES

Plants that help

Home remedies

One tree, on average, can make up to **300,000** pencils!

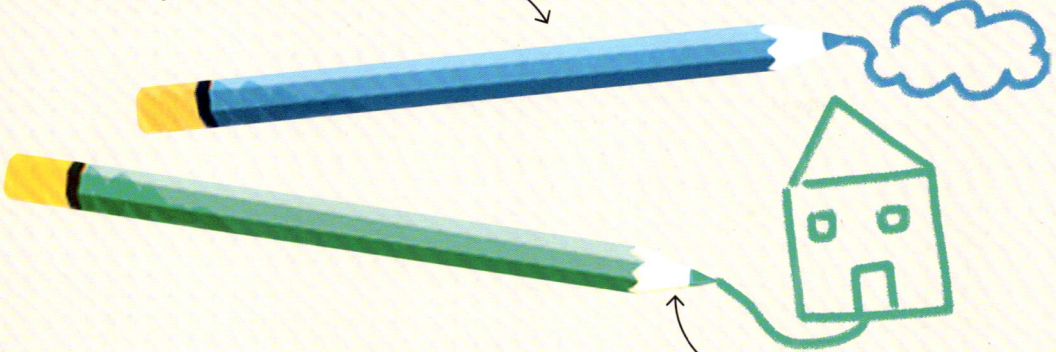

Most pencils are made from cedar trees.

Apples, pears and cherries are all part of the rose family.

A sunflower has loads of tiny flowers called florets which ripen to become the seeds. You can eat these seeds!

90% of food that humans eat comes from **30** plants!

Match Up the Pairs

Can you match up the fact boxes (below) with the correct plant (right)?
Flip back through the book if you need a hint!

1.

I'm a fluffy, white flower which can be turned into thread and used to make clothes.

2.

I'm a plant eaten by pandas. Humans use me to build houses, furniture, and even make toothbrushes!

3.

I'm a pretty flower which can be turned into a cancer-fighting medicine.

4.

I'm a flowering plant. I may be pretty, but I'm very poisonous, so don't touch me!

5.

I'm a spicy fruit which is used in cooking to add "heat" to food.

6.

My green leaves are used as a herb in cooking all over the world.

Chili pepper

Foxgloves

Bamboo

Basil plant

Cotton

Rose periwinkle

Have you matched them all?
Answers can be found on page 24.

Glossary

Bark – the tough outer layer of a woody plant stem or root, such as a tree trunk.

Bulbs – rounded parts of some plants that grow in the soil. They store food and shoots grow out of them.

Camouflage – to look like something else in order to stay hidden.

Carbon dioxide – an invisible gas in the air that plants take in to make food and oxygen.

Diet – food that you eat regularly.

Droughts – a long period of dryness, usually caused by lack of rainfall.

Evergreen - a type of plant whose leaves stay green all year round. These plants also do not lose their leaves in winter.

Flooding – when large amounts of water overflows into areas of land where it shouldn't be.

Global warming – the rising temperature of the planet, which causes climate change.

Habitats – the natural homes of plants and animals.

Herbivore – an animal that only eats plants.

Nutrients – substances or ingredients that plants and animals need to live and grow.

Oxygen – an invisible gas in the air that plants produce, and people and animals need to breathe.

Pollute – (verb) to make dirty or harmful with waste, chemicals, or other substances.

Sap – a watery substance that comes out of a plant or tree.

Trunk – the large woody stem of a tree, where the branches grow from.

Answers to Match Up the Pairs

Answers: 1. Cotton, 2. Bamboo, 3. Rose periwinkle, 4. Foxgloves, 5. Chili pepper, 6. Basil plant.